BOOK OF POEMS
FOR ENCOURAGEMENT

Earl M. Tillis

DEDICATION

To my beloved wife, Ana, and my children, EJ and Justin, and my daughter-laws Genesis, and Tasheana. Your unwavering support and endless encouragement have been the bedrock of my journey. Together, we have faced life's challenges and celebrated its joys, always standing strong as a family. I am deeply grateful for each of you and cherish the love that binds us together. This book is a testament to our unity and the love that sustains us.

With all my heart, Earl Tillis

ACKNOWLEDGMENT

I would like to express my deepest gratitude to everyone who has encouraged and supported me on this journey. To my family and friends, your unwavering belief in me has been a constant source of inspiration. To my mentors and fellow brothers and sisters, your wisdom and guidance have helped shape these words into the verses they are today. Lastly, to my readers, thank you for opening your hearts to what God has stirred in my heart. Your encouragement fuels my passion and creativity. This book is dedicated to all who believe in the power of words Trusting the God who created us all.

CONTENTS

ABOUT THE AUTHOR

Earl M. Tillis Sr. is an inspiring author who has faced and over-come significant challenges in his life. After losing his eyesight, Earl's journey became a testament to the power of faith and resilience. Through his book "When the Lights Went Out," and "The Storm Is Not Over Yet" and now his new book, a "Book Of Poems For Encouragement" inspirers us to never give up. He shares his personal story of hardship, perseverance, and trust in God. Earl's unwavering faith and determination to adapt to his new reality have not only helped him navigate the difficulties of losing his sight but also enabled him to inspire and encourage others facing similar trials. His story is a powerful reminder of the strength that can be found in trusting a higher power and the human spirit's capacity to overcome adversity.

Earl M. Tillis

<u>INTRODUCTION</u>

In this collection of heartfelt reflections and poems, I invite you to join me on a journey of faith and inspiration. Life is filled with moments of joy and triumph, but it also presents us with challenges and uncertainties. Yet, through it all, there is a guiding light that illuminates our path— the unwavering love and promises of God.

In these pages, I share personal experiences and lessons learned, offering encouragement and hope to those facing their own trials and struggles. Each poem and reflection is a testament to the faithfulness of God and the transformative power of His grace.

May these words uplift your spirit, renew your strength, and remind you of the enduring truth that, even in the midst of darkness, the dawn of hope awaits. As we journey together through these pages, may you discover a deeper sense of peace and assurance in the everlasting love of our Creator.

Let us embark on this journey of faith, where the echoes of encouragement resonate and inspire us to press on, knowing that the best is yet to come.

With hope and faith,

Earl M. Tillis

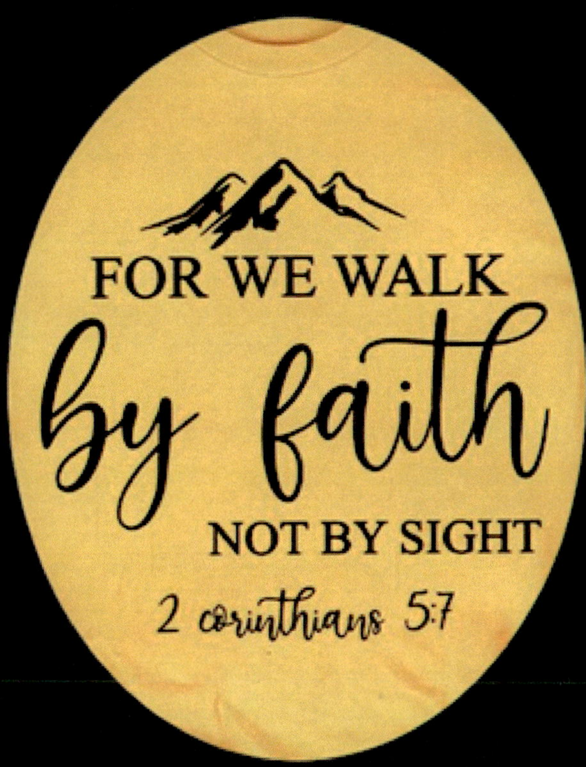

It is by faith I realize that there is safety in His arms

VISION BEYOND SIGHT

Though darkness veils my earthly eyes,
And shadows hide the world from view,
In faith, I see with heart and soul,
The light of Christ, forever true.
Though outward sight may fade away,
Inward vision grows more clear,
For God reveals His wondrous love,
In ways unseen, yet ever near.

In Christ my Savior I abide,
His Word a lamp unto my feet,
Guiding me through life's unknown paths,
With trust and courage, strong and sweet.
For in His presence, darkness flees,
And fear gives way to perfect peace,
His Spirit whispers in the night,
Assuring me of His release.

Though eyes may not behold the dawn,
I sense the beauty of His grace,
In melodies of birds that sing,
In gentle whispers of His embrace.
For God's creation speaks of Him,
In vibrant colors sounds and signs,
His majesty and glory shine,
In every moment, for all time.

So I will praise Him with my soul,
With heart attuned to heaven's song,
For in His love I am made whole,
In His embrace I do belong.
Though earthly eyes may not perceive,
The wonders of this world so bright,
My spirit soars on wings of faith,
To realms of joy and heavenly light.

One day in glory I shall see,
The face of Christ my King and Lord,
And in His presence ever free,
Rejoice in heaven's great reward.

Scripture teaches that it's OK to get angry, but it comes with a condition.

Be ye angry, and sin not: let not the sun go down upon your wrath: 27 Neither give place to the devil. 28 Let him that stole steal no more: but rather let him labour, working with his hands the thing which is good, that he may have to give to him that needeth. Ephesians 4:26 28

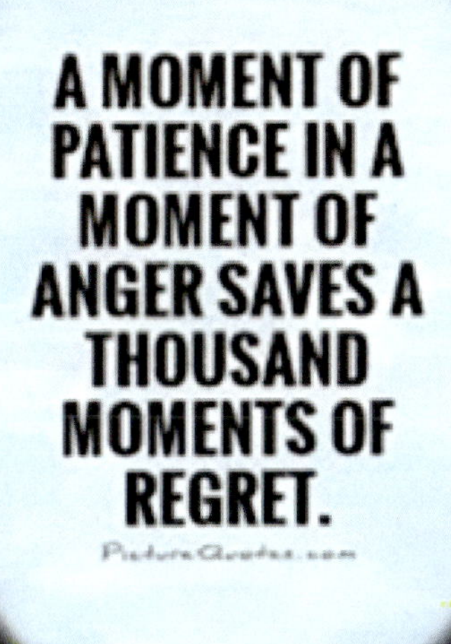

FINDING PEACE IN ANGER

In moments of anger, when storms rage within,
And questions arise, asking where to begin,
I lift up my voice to the God of all grace,
Pouring out my heart in this sacred space.

Lord I confess, I am angry and torn,
Feeling lost and adrift, my heart deeply worn,
Yet in the midst of my doubts and my pain,
You remain steadfast, Your love does sustain.

You understand my anguish, my every thought,
You hold me close, though my heart feels distraught,
For You are a God, who welcomes our cries,
You listen in love, though the tears fill our eyes.

Help me O Lord, to surrender this weight,
To trust in Your wisdom, to patiently wait,
For Your ways are higher, Your thoughts beyond mine,
In surrender may Your peace, in me shine.

Though anger may linger, and doubts may persist,
In Your presence O God, my soul finds its rest,
For You are the Anchor, that steadies my soul,
In Your arms of mercy, I am made whole.

Renew my faith O Lord, in Your perfect plan,
May my heart be open, to Your guiding hand,
Help me see beyond, this moment of pain,
To embrace Your love, in sunshine and rain.

For even in anger, Your grace does abound,
In the depths of my soul, Your peace can be found,
So I surrender my heart, my will and my fear,
Knowing that in You, I am always held dear.

HOPE IS BEING ABLE TO SEE
THAT THERE IS LIGHvT DESPITE
ALL OF THE DARKNESS

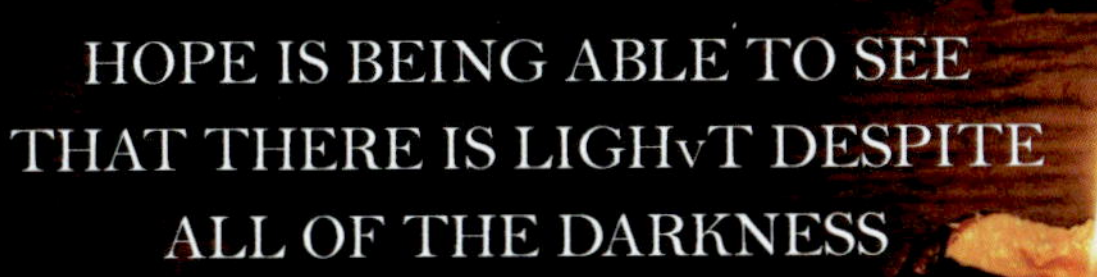

" I can see clearly, now that the pain has gone away"

HOPE IN THE DARKNESS

In the depths of despair, where shadows loom,
And darkness seems, to fill the silent room,
Hold onto hope, let faith be your guide,
For God is near, He walks by your side.

Though sadness grips, your weary soul,
And waves of sorrow, take their toll,
Know that you are not alone, in this fight,
God sees your pain, and holds you tight.

When hope feels far away, like a distant star,
Remember, His love reaches where you are,
He heals the brokenhearted, binds up the wound,
In His presence, new beginnings are cocooned.

Turn to Him in prayer, pour out your heart,
For He listens closely, to every part,
His peace surpasses, all understanding,
Bringing comfort, to the depths demanding.

You are precious, and valued beyond measure,
A masterpiece crafted, with divine treasure,
In God's eyes, you are wonderfully made,
With a purpose, that cannot be swayed.

Take one step forward, then another still,
As His grace empowers, you with His will,
Though the journey may seem, steep and long,
In His strength you'll rise, and you'll be strong.

Hold onto faith, let hope be your song,
For the night may be dark, but joy comes with the dawn,
Trust in the Lord, let His light lead the way,
For His love conquers all, day by day.

MY JOURNEY WITH JESUS

When is the last time your had a walk with Jesus

THE JOURNEY WITH HIM

Each day begins, with morning light,
A gift of grace a brand-new sight,
We rise and seek the One above,
To walk with Him in faith and love.
In quiet moments hearts are still,
To hear His voice to know His will,

Through open Word and whispered prayer,
He meets us with His tender care.
He walks beside us through each hour,
In valleys low and mountains tower,
His presence steady, strong, and true,
Guiding our steps in all we do.

When trials come and fears surround,
His peace descends a holy ground,
For in His hands we find our rest,
In every trial we are blessed.
He teaches us to trust His ways,
To follow Him through endless days,

To serve with love and humble grace,
Reflecting Him in every place.
And as we journey, hand in hand,
With Christ, our Savior, King, and Friend,
We find our purpose, joy, and worth,
In Him, the Author of our birth.

So let us walk with hearts ablaze,
In His love, be lost in praise,
For every step, each breath we take,
Is filled with His amazing grace.
May our daily walk with Christ inspire,
Hearts set on things that never tire,
Until we reach our home above,
Forever walking in His love.

SOMETIMES YOUR JOY IS THE SOURCE OF YOUR TEARS SOMETIMES YOUR SMILE CAN BE THE SOURCE OF YOUR JOY

Weeping may endure for a night but joy comes in the morning

TEARS OF JOY

In moments sweet and sacred tears flow free,
As I stand in awe of Your great love for me,
Oh Lord Your grace is like an endless sea,
Overflowing with mercy boundless and free.

Tears of joy stream down my face,
As I'm captivated by Your amazing grace,
You rescued me from sin's dark place,
And filled my heart with Your embrace.

In the silence of Your presence I find peace,
Every burden lifted every worry released,
Your love surrounds me like a gentle breeze,
Bringing comfort and hope and sweet relief.

I am overwhelmed by Your faithfulness,
Your promises hold true in every test,
You are my strength, my refuge, and fortress,
In Your love I am forever blessed.

Oh how wonderful is Your unfailing love,
A gift from heaven descending like a dove,
It lifts me high on wings of joyful praise,
To worship You with all my days.

So I lift my voice in songs of adoration,
Grateful for Your boundless salvation,
With tears of joy I proclaim Your name,
For Your love forever remains the same.

Thank You Lord for Your redeeming grace,
For the joy that shines upon my face,
In Your presence I find my eternal place,
Forever held by Your loving embrace.

I have been crucified with Christ

It is no longer I who lives, but Christ lives in me Galatians 2:20

A MAN'S SURRENDER

In the stillness of the morning,
As the world begins to wake,
There's a stirring deep within,
A soul that longs to seek and take.
A man stands at the crossroads,
Where paths diverge left and right,
But in the silence of his heart,
He feels a call to inner light.

No longer bound by pride or fear,
He kneels before the King of Kings,
With trembling hands and humbled heart,
He surrenders all that life brings.
To You, O Lord, he speaks in earnest,
"Take my heart, my soul, my all,
For I am nothing without Your grace,
I surrender at Your loving call."

In brokenness, he finds strength,
In surrender true freedom's key,
For God's embrace is warm and wide,
Welcoming him eternally.
No longer striving on his own,
But anchored in God's steadfast love,
He walks in faith his heart transformed,
Reflecting the glory from above.

O men, arise and heed the call,
To yield your lives to God's embrace,
For in surrender you will find,
Abundant joy and lasting grace.
Give Him your heart your very soul,
Let Him reign on heaven's throne,
For in surrendering all to Him,
You'll find your true self fully known.

The Lord is not slow in keeping his promise, as some understand slowness.

Instead he is patient with you, not wanting anyone to perish,...

2 Peter 3:9

STRENGTH IN TRIALS

Dear sister, when the storms of life draw near,
And trials and tribulations cause you fear,
Remember, you are not alone in this fight,
For God is with you His love shining bright.
Though hardships may seem too heavy to bear,
Know that God's strength is beyond compare,

He lifts you up on wings like eagles' flight,
Giving you courage and unwavering might.
In the midst of trials your faith is refined,
Like gold tested by fire beautifully designed,
For God is working in ways you can't see
Molding you into who He meant you to be.

Take heart dear sister and do not lose hope,
For God's promises are your steadfast rope,
He will never leave you nor forsake,
In His embrace find refuge and strength to partake.
Through every trial trust His perfect plan,
He will turn your mourning into joy again,

Your tears He collects in His bottle divine,
And in His time, radiant victory will shine.
So hold onto hope keep your eyes above,
Where God's grace flows in unending love,
For in Christ you are more than conquerors. you see,
Victorious in Him through eternity.

All of creation is a
song of praise to God.

IN PRAISE OF CREATION

Behold the beauty all around,
In nature's canvas colors abound,
From mountains high to oceans wide,
God's handiwork a wondrous tide.

The skies declare His glory bright,
With stars that twinkle in the night,
The sun that rises warm and gold,
A daily promise ages old.

In forests deep where creatures roam,
Each one a testament of His home,
From smallest ant to soaring eagle,
God's creation vast and regal.

The gentle breeze that whispers soft,
The mighty waves that crash aloft,
The fields adorned with flowers bright,
Revealing God's creative might.

Oh, let us marvel and adore,
The wonders God has set before,
For in His creation, we can see,
His love and grace eternally.

Each creature each leaf each blade of grass,
A part of His grand divine class,
In harmony they all proclaim,
The greatness of His holy name.

So let us cherish let us care,
For every living thing with prayer,
And in God's creation let us find,
A reflection of His heart so kind.
For all was made by His decree,
To show His love abundantly,
In awe and wonder let us sing,
For all creation that he brings.

Thanking
God
in SICKNESS
& in HEALTH

IN THE SHADOW OF ILLNESS

In the shadow of illness when hope seems thin,
Remember Hezekiah, the faithful king within,
Facing death's door he sought the Lord's face,
With prayers and tears he found God's saving grace.
"Set your house in order," the prophet did say,
But Hezekiah turned to God without delay,

He cried out in anguish with faith unswayed,
And God heard his plea, a miraculous display.
A promise of healing a sign in the sky,
A sundial's shadow moved back so high,
For God's mercy and power, nothing is too great,
Hezekiah's life extended, by divine fate.

So take heart dear one, in your time of trial,
For God's love and compassion will never defile,
He sees your suffering, He hears every prayer,
In His perfect timing, He answers with care.
In the face of uncertainty trust in His plan,
Lean on His promises for they firmly stand,

Like Hezekiah, seek God's face anew,
And watch Him work wonders, bringing life into view.
For His ways are higher, His thoughts beyond ours,
In weakness His strength, does empower,
Hold onto hope let faith rise above,
For God is the healer of hearts, the giver of love.

Lord Give Me
Faith Like Daniel In The Lion's Den
Hope Like Moses In The Wilderness
And A Heart Like David
So I Can Face My Gaints
With Confidence

A HEART LIKE DAVID'S

In ancient times of old, a shepherd boy arose,
A heart so true and bold, with love that freely flows,
His name was David, chosen by the Lord above,
A man after God's own heart, filled with grace and love.
With courage and faith, he faced the giant's might,
Trusting in God alone, he won the victor's fight,

A humble servant-king, with melodies of praise,
In joyful songs and psalms, his heart to God he'd raise.
Through trials and triumphs, his faith remained secure,
In valleys dark and deep, God's presence was his cure,
For David knew the secret, to seek the Lord each day,
In prayer and supplication, he'd humbly kneel and pray.

Oh for a heart like David's, passionate and true,
A heart that longs for God, in all we say and do,
To love Him with abandon, to follow His commands,
To trust His perfect wisdom, and rest in His strong hands.
May David's legacy inspire us, to seek the Lord with zeal,
To walk in righteousness, and His great love reveal,

For in a heart surrendered, God's glory shines so bright,
May we be like David, hearts aflame with heavenly light.
So let us fix our eyes on Jesus, the Author of our faith,
And emulate the heart of David today, and don't wait,
With faith like his, unwavering and strong,
May we live for God's glory, our hearts forever His song.

The steadfast love of the LORD never ceases, his mercies never come to an end; they are new every morning; great is your faithfulness.

STEADFAST LOVE

When shadows deepen, and doubts arise,
I lift my gaze to the radiant skies,
For in the heavens my help is found,
In God's embrace my soul is bound.

I can count on God, in every storm,
His faithfulness, an anchor conformed,
Through trials and triumphs, He is near,
To calm my fears and dry each tear.

When burdens weigh and hope seems dim,
I find strength within, cause I trust in Him,
His promises, like pillars strong and true,
Guide me forward, His mercies anew.

In times of need, I seek His face,
And He provides with boundless grace,
For He is faithful, forevermore,
A constant refuge, my heart's restore.

So I will lean on His steadfast love,
For He's the One I can always count on,
In every season, He remains the same,
My Rock, my Redeemer, in His name.

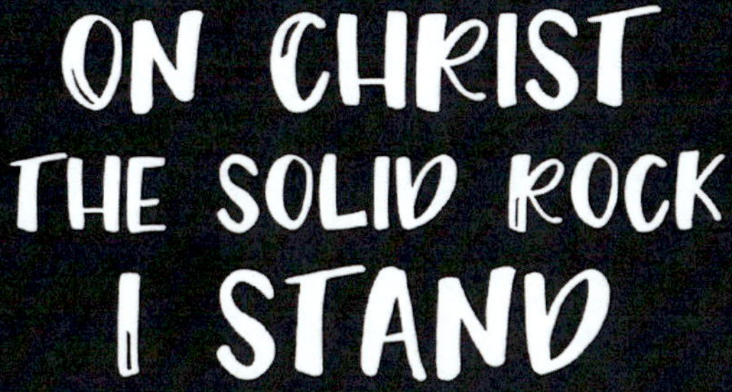
ON CHRIST
THE SOLID ROCK
I STAND
ALL OTHER GROUND
IS SINKING SAND

STANDING FIRM ON HIS WORD

In the beginning, spoken with power divine,
The Word of God, a radiant light did shine,
From age to age, its truth resounds,
A steadfast anchor, where hope abounds.

In pages written, a timeless scroll unfurled,
Revealing God's heart, to a searching world,
Each word a promise, each verse a guiding star,
To lead us home, no matter how far.

In every trial, in every storm we face,
The Word stands firm, a rock and hiding place,
Its wisdom whispers, through the winds of time,
A lamp unto our feet, a path sublime.

Through joy and sorrow, in each season's turn,
The Word of God, our hearts and minds discern,
It comforts, strengthens, and revives the soul,
Pointing us to Jesus, our Savior whole.

So cherish this treasure, this gift divine,
The everlasting Word, a holy sign,
For heaven and earth will pass away,
But God's Word endures, forever to stay.

And be not conformed
to this
World but be
TRANSFORMED
by the
Renewing
OF MIND
YOUR
that you may prove what is that
good, and acceptable, and perfect,
WILL of GOD.

ROMANS 12:2

RENEW MY MIND

Renew my mind O Lord this day,
With truths that never fade away,
Unveil Your wisdom pure and bright,
To guide my thoughts in Your pure light.

Remove the doubts that cloud my soul,
Replace with faith that makes me whole,
Let every word I think or say,
Reflect Your love in every way.

Renew my spirit breathe Your life,
With strength to conquer doubt and strife,
Ignite the fire within my heart,
To boldly live out every part.

Revive my passion for Your ways,
In worship and in prayer and praise,
May joy and peace in me abound,
As Your Spirit's grace is found.

Renew my soul O God of grace,
In Your presence let me embrace,
The fullness of Your love divine,
A steadfast anchor truly mine.

May Your truth resound within my being,
In every moment ever freeing,
Renew me daily Lord I pray,
To walk in Your light each step of the way.

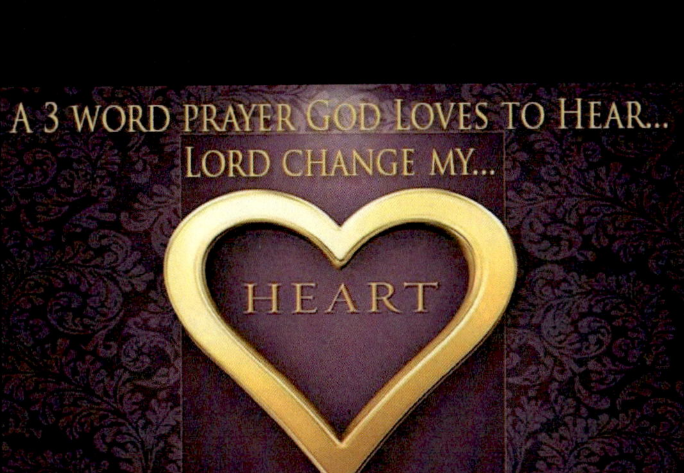
A 3 WORD PRAYER GOD LOVES TO HEAR...
LORD CHANGE MY...
HEART
PSALM 119:10

With my whole heart I seek you; do not let me stray from
your commandments.

LORD HUMBLE MY HEART

In the quiet of this sacred hour,
I lift my voice to You O Lord,
With humble heart and spirit bowed,
I come before your throne adored.

Father hear my earnest plea,
For you alone can satisfy,
You know the depths of all I need,
In your presence let me abide.

Grant me wisdom, strength, and grace,
To face each trial, each unknown,
Fill me with your perfect peace,
In your presence, I am not alone.

Guide my steps along your way,
Illuminate the path ahead,
Let your Word be my guiding light,
And your Spirit my daily bread.

Lord I trust your perfect plan,
Though mysteries may cloud my sight,
Help me walk by faith each day,
In your promises my soul takes flight.

May your will be done in me,
As in heaven, so on earth,
Let Your kingdom reign in power,
Through my life a witness of your worth.

Thank you Father for your love,
For the privilege to seek your face,
In prayer and praise, my heart is lifted,
In your presence, I find peace and grace.

Just when you think you know what Love is...
along come the Grandchildren

GOD'S GIFT

As seasons turn and years unfold,
A precious gift you now behold,
For in your arms a grandchild sweet,
A miracle of life pure and complete.

Oh what joy to see this little one,
A testament of God's love, like the rising sun,
In innocent laughter and tender embrace,
Feel Heaven's touch God's wondrous grace.

As you hold this precious life so dear,
Whisper prayers of blessing loud and clear,
For God's plans for them are vast and wide,
Guided by His love forever by their side.

May you share with them the truths you know,
Of faith and hope that forever grow,
In your love may they see God's light,
A beacon shining pure and bright.

So cherish this role this special place,
As a grandparent filled with love and grace,
For in each moment God's blessings flow,
As generations flourish His goodness to show.

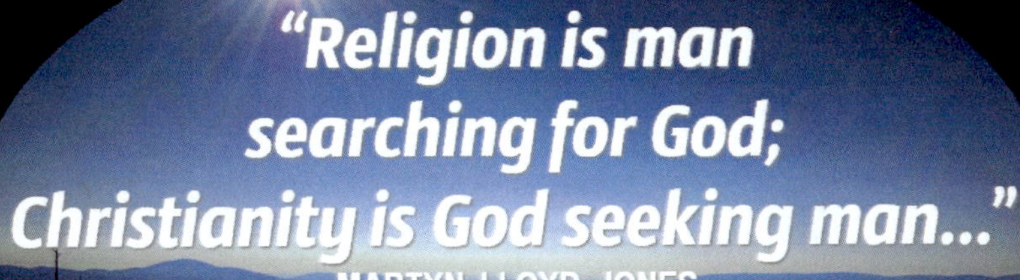

"Religion is man searching for God; Christianity is God seeking man..."
-MARTYN LLOYD JONES
"No one can come to Me unless the Father who sent Me draws him; and I will raise him up at the last day." (John 6:44)

SEARCHING FOR GOD

In the depths of yearning where shadows loom,
A soul seeks solace in the quiet room,
Longing for a glimpse of the Divine,
Searching for God in a sacred shrine.

Through winding paths and valleys low,
Where doubts may linger and fears may grow,
There echoes a voice soft and clear,
Drawing the seeker ever near.

In whispered prayers and silent cries,
In starlit nights and morning skies,
God's presence lingers gentle and true,
Revealing Himself in ways anew.

In sacred texts and ancient lore,
In nature's beauty His glory soars,
Seek and you shall find the promise holds,
For He reveals Himself to seeking souls.

Embrace the journey with faith and trust,
In the quest for God let love be your compass,
For in seeking Him you'll surely see,
His loving and caring love for me.

Streams of
Living Water

"If anyone is thirsty, let
him come to me."

John 7:37b-38

SOMETHING IN THE WATER

Walking by faith not by sight,
In the depths of doubt's darkest night,
But there's something in the water,
A stirring of hope, a love that won't falter.

Dive into grace, let fear be washed away,
In the river of mercy, where shadows sway,
Feel the cleansing tide, like a newborn daughter or son,
Baptized in His love, a new life begun.

Oh there must be something in the water,
Changing hearts, setting souls free,
In the waves of redemption, find your destiny,
Rise up oh soul, let your spirit soar,
For there's something in the water, forevermore.

In the ebb and flow of life's winding stream,
Let faith arise, like a radiant dream,
Miracles unfold, in the depths so wide,
In the living water, where love abides.

So take the plunge, let your heart be transformed,
In the currents of grace, where hope is reborn,
There's a river of healing, a divine embrace,
For there's something in the water, God's amazing grace.

LET US
Hold Fast
THE CONFESSION
of our
HOPE
WITHOUT
Wavering
FOR HE WHO
PROMISED
HEB. is faithful 10:23

HOLD FAST TO HOPE

When doubts arise and faith feels weak,
Hold fast to hope, let your spirit speak,
For in the silence, God's voice is near,
Whispering promises of love sincere.

Believe in miracles, both big and small,
In unseen hands that catch us when we fall,
For God works wonders, beyond our sight,
Turning darkness into radiant light.

Trust in His timing, though it may be slow,
His ways are perfect, His love will show,
The impossible becomes reality,
When faith unlocks His boundless majesty.

Look to the heavens, where stars proclaim,
The wonders of His glory and His name,
In every heartbeat, in each breath you take,
See His miracles unfold, never forsake.

So stand in awe of His miraculous might,
With childlike wonder, embrace the light,
For in believing, you receive His grace,
And miracles abound in every place.

Search for peace
and you will not find it,
but search for God
and you will find peace.

HIS GRACE

In the silence of the morning tide,
Where whispers of faith softly reside,
I find assurance in His steadfast grace,
Why God fights battles in our place.

Though trials assail and fears surround,
In His love, a fortress strong and sound,
He goes before us, in every fray,
His mighty hand leads us each day.

For His ways are higher, His wisdom deep,
In every struggle, His promises keep,
He fights our battles with strength untold,
To show His power, His truth uphold.

It's not by strength or human might,
But by His Spirit, radiant and bright,
That victories are won, against all odds,
In His embrace, we find our peace in God.

the joy
of
the LORD
is my
strength
Nehemiah 8:10

NOT BY OUR STRENGTH

In the vast expanse of life's winding road,
There shines a grace, a mercy untold,
Where trials loom and burdens seem too great,
By God's own hand, our souls to elevate.

Not by our strength, but His unfailing love,
In every challenge, His grace soars above,
We find solace, in the midst of strife,
Sustaining us with hope, for a new life.

Through darkest valleys, He walks by our side,
With arms outstretched, His grace becomes our guide,
His light breaking through the shadows of despair,
To lift us up and show us He is there.

Oh, the depth and richness of His grace,
Embracing every heart in its warm embrace,
A river flowing from eternity's throne,
Assuring us we'll never walk alone.

So take courage weary soul, and do not fear,
In His strength and love, find your purpose clear,
For God's grace is more than sufficient to endure,
For His grace is endless, His mercy ever sure.

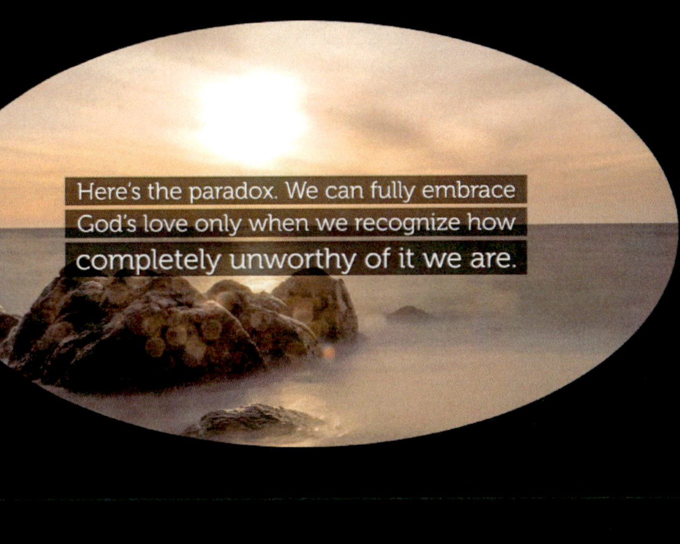
Here's the paradox. We can fully embrace
God's love only when we recognize how
completely unworthy of it we are.

SACRIFICE OF LOVE

Behold the love that knows no bounds,
A love that reaches depths profound,
From realms above to earthly ground,
God's love in Christ, forever crowned.

In tender mercy, He gave His Son,
To bear our sins, the victory won,
Upon the cross, redemption won come,
Through Jesus Christ, the chosen One.

No greater love could ever be,
Than Christ's own death to set us free,
To reconcile us, you and me,
In Him, we find true liberty.

Though storms may rage and tempests roar,
His love remains forevermore,
A steadfast anchor, strong and sure,
In Him, our hearts find peace secure.

So let this love, O soul embrace,
And marvel at its boundless grace,
In every trial, in every place,
God's love endures, a saving embrace.

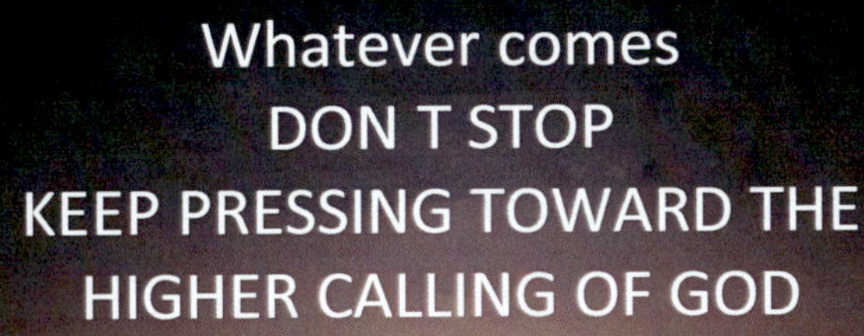

DON'T STOP, PRESS ON

In the crucible of life's fiery trials,
Yet in the furnace, hope gently smiles,
A man walks through valleys deep and wide,
For God walks beside him, faithful guide.

When burdens weigh heavy upon his frame,
He lifts his eyes to the One who came,
And doubts assail like waves upon the shore,
To carry his load and so much more.

For strength arises from surrendered will,
Each struggle shapes him, refining still,
In weakness, God's power is made complete,
A vessel of grace, forged by mercy sweet.

Though storms may rage and shadows loom large,
In Christ he finds refuge, a mighty charge,
His faith stands firm on the Rock unyielding,
To overcome, with courage ever building.

So press on, oh man of steadfast heart,
You're never alone; He'll never depart,
For in your journey, God's glory shines,
In Him your hope, your peace entwines.

Jesus
Can Restore Your Life!

THE CROSS

Upon the cross, where love's pure essence bled,
Jesus the Lamb, in grace and mercy led,
A sacrifice unmatched, for all to see,
Gave life for us, to set our spirits free.

Oh wondrous gift, this act of boundless grace,
Through crimson streams, our sins He erase,
Where heaven's light embraced humanity,
To grant us life and hope eternally.

In darkest hours, when shadows veil the way,
His cross a beacon through the night and day,
Remember Him who bore our every pain,
Declares that victory shall rise again.

No greater love has ever been displayed,
In resurrection's dawn, all debts are paid,
Than Christ's own death upon that rugged tree,
Salvation's song rings out, forever free.

So lift your eyes, behold the empty grave,
In Christ our Savior mighty to save,
For in His rising, find your victory,
Restored, renewed, in His sweet majesty.

IF
GOD
IS FOR US
WHO CAN BE
Against us?
ROMANS 8:31

GOD IS WITH U

In shadows deep, when hope's a distant gleam,
Hold fast to faith, though skies may not yet beam,
And trials loom like mountains in the way,
For strength abides where hearts in prayer stay.

The path may wind through valleys low and still,
In whispers soft or through a tempest shrill,
Yet know that God walks with you every stride,
His love surrounds, a fortress by your side.

When tears fall freely in the silent night,
Seek solace in His everlasting light,
And fears like thunder echo through the soul,
Where grace and peace can mend and make you whole.

For storms will pass, though now fierce they roar,
Embrace the journey, trust in Him once more,
And joy will rise with morning's golden ray,
For faith endures beyond each night and day.

So take heart weary traveler on this road,
For God our refuge, bears our heavy load,
Let courage bloom amidst the thorns of pain,
And in His arms, new hope is born again.

GOD'S MASTERPIECE

WHO R U ?

In the eyes of God, you are fearfully made,
Chosen and cherished, in His image displayed,
A masterpiece crafted by His loving hand,
With a purpose divine, uniquely planned.

You are not forgotten, nor lost in the crowd,
In your joys and struggles, God's love is endowed,
But known intimately, every thought and deed,
A beacon of hope for every soul in need.

In His eyes you're precious, worth more than gold,
Redeemed by the blood that was willingly sold,
A treasure held close to His heart of grace,
In the vastness of, His mercy-filled embrace.

So lift up your head, let your spirit soar high,
In His presence, find peace that will never die,
For you are beloved, a child of the King,
And let His praises through your life ring.

For in the eyes of God, you are wonderfully seen,
You are His creation, radiant and serene,
Embrace His love, His purpose and His plan,
In His eternal kingdom, forever you'll stand.

"WALKING BY FAITH"

is a metaphorical phrase that means

"TO LIVE OR MAKE A HABIT OF LIVING BASED ON FAITH AND NOT SIGHT."

It's often used in reference to 2 Corinthians 5:7, which says, "For we walk by faith, not by sight". This verse suggests that people who walk by faith have an eternal perspective and believe so strongly in the gospel that their struggles are not their main concern.

Affirmation: **The wonders of His love**
Scripture: Psalm 139:14 (NIV)
"I praise you because I am fearfully and wonderfully made; your works are wonderful, I know that full well."

Affirmation: **In His Strength**
Scripture: Philippians 4:13 (NKJV)
"I can do all things through Christ who strengthens me."

Affirmation: **He is my provider**
Scripture: Psalm 23:1 (NIV)
"The Lord is my shepherd, I lack nothing."

Affirmation: **I overcome through His strength**
Scripture: Romans 8:37 (NIV)
"No, in all these things we are more than conquerors through him who loved us."

Affirmation: **God's plan is to prosper you**
Scripture: Jeremiah 29:11 (NLT)
"For I know the plans I have for you," says the Lord. "They are plans for good and not for disaster, to give you a future and a hope."

Affirmation: **God's blessings follow me**
Scripture: Deuteronomy 28:6 (NIV)
"You will be blessed when you come in and blessed when you go out."

Affirmation: **Created for great things**
Scripture: Ephesians 2:10 (NIV)
"For we are God's handiwork, created in Christ Jesus to do good works, which God prepared in advance for us to do."

Affirmation: **He made me strong and courageous**
Scripture: Joshua 1:9 (NIV)
"Have I not commanded you? Be strong and courageous. Do not be afraid; do not be discouraged, for the Lord your God will be with you wherever you go."

Affirmation: **Lord make me over**
Scripture: 2 Corinthians 5:17 (NIV)
"Therefore, if anyone is in Christ, the new creation has come: The old has gone, the new is here!"

Affirmation: **I am strengthen through Christ**
Scripture: Nehemiah 8:10 (NIV)
"Do not grieve, for the joy of the Lord is your strength."

Affirmation: **I am a child of God.**
Scripture: John 1:12 (NIV)
"Yet to all who did receive him, to those who believed in his name, he gave the right to become children of God."

Affirmation: **God will give you more then what you ask for**
Scripture: Ephesians 3:20 (NIV)
"Now to him who is able to do immeasurably more than all we ask or imagine, according to his power that is at work within us."

In closing, may these heartfelt encouragements serve as a gentle whispers of hope and resilience in your journey through life's highs and lows. Let these words resonate within you, reminding you of the strength that resides in your heart and the boundless possibilities that awaits you. As you turn the final pages of this book, may you carry its messages with you, uplifting yourself and others with each step forward. Remember, you are capable, you are worthy, and you are loved. Embrace each new day with courage and kindness, knowing that within you lies the power to shine brightly and inspire others.

Earl M. Tillis